Fire Baton

Poems by
Elizabeth Hadaway

The University of Arkansas Press

Fayetteville

2006

Text design by Ellen Beeler

Library of Congress Cataloging-in-Publication Data
Hadaway, Elizabeth, 1968–
    Fire baton : poems / by Elizabeth Hadaway.
        p. cm.
    ISBN 1-55728-824-0 (pbk. : alk. paper)
    I. Title.
    PS3608.A257F57 2006
    811'.6—dc22

                                                    2006017523

to the memory of Walter Wesley Palmer

Acknowledgments

Grateful acknowledgments to the following publications, in which these poems have appeared, some under the name Leigh Palmer:

"Idol Meat" (as "Miss Osbourne to the Telemarketer"), "Beating My Head on a Curb in California" (as "Police Radio Remembered"), *Ambo;* "Amazed at Gray Light," *Anglican Theological Review;* "Drinking Bottled Water," *Appalachian Heritage;* "Ghosts for Dinner," *The Bellingham Review;* "Magic City Mortgage Co., 1951" (as "Lee Highway, 1950"), *The Blue Penny Quarterly;* "All Short-*a* Appalachia," "Living with the Bureau of Public Debt," *DIAGRAM;* "Silicon Valley, 1998," *Emrys Journal;* "Faculty Parking Apocalypse" (as "Pavementscape"), *The Enterprise;* "Disney Ride *Song of the South,*" *Five Fingers Review;* "Crop Cults" (as "She Tries to Narrow Down His Doubts"), *Greensboro Review;* "A Scratch," *New England Review;* "Was You Born Here?" "Living with Ballads: Sidna Allen," "The Black Dog of the Blue Ridge," *Poetry;* "The Black Dog of the Blue Ridge" (on January 28, 2005, by permission of *Poetry*), *Poetry Daily;* "Richmond Breastworks" (as "Ode to the Dodger Dead"), *Shenandoah;* and "The Banks of Hell" (as "Hook, Line"), *Yale Anglers' Journal.*

"The Shower Curtain Swans" rotated as a Public Service Poem on WTJU Radio (Charlottesville, Virginia).

Thanks also to my mother, my husband, all my teachers, Enid Shomer for her editing, Carolyn Brady, Poppy Z. Brite, Jennifer Buxton, Margo Figgins, Maria Hagan, Matthew Kirsch, Elizabeth Seydel Morgan, Tara Moyle, Browning Porter, Wendy Shang, the University of North Carolina at Greensboro, Stanford University, Virginia Theological Seminary, the Bread Loaf Writers' Conference, the Sewanee Writers' Conference, and the University of Virginia's Young Writers' Workshop.

Contents

Fire Baton

Was You Born Here?

"Cause you don't talk like you
was born here," said
my probable fourth cousin,
at least an eighth. "Coarse-bred,"

Yeats called Cockney Keats. What
he'd think of me I know.
I'm talking American Viscose,
Magic City Mortgage Co.

among my parentage.
But marry that
to old moonshiners who read Cicero.
In nothing flat—

in rounded mountains, knobs
where *where*'s *whirr,* peaks
of laurel burning into bloom—
I start to speak,

sound like a stranger everywhirr.
The Cure taught me Camus
and still the flatland bouncer asks,
"You're *from* somewhere, aren't you?"

All Short-*a* Appalachia

You want to ratchet this world's fury down?
Then learn to say it right. Not Appa-*lay*-
cha, Appa-*latch*-a. This means you,
you NPR announcers earnestly
enunciating all the accent marks
in Spanish or Sanskrit, you editors
who grant the standard and nonstandard tags
in dictionaries.
                    No, you didn't trash
our water, gash and snatch the mountaintops,
eradicate the chestnut trees, or plan
the factory stacks personally. You
just trample out our vowels.
                            Hear the whole
diaspora slam down their beer cans, stab
their classes' final drafts, and smash the half-
carved radishes before they've had a chance
to bloom as radish roses?
                        We do that
as often as the quack newscasters drag
their "Appa-lay-cha" out.
                        It's not like quaint
or paid.
        It's short *a*: acid, ash, scab, smack,
catastrophe, Cassandra, slag, last, wrath.

The Black Dog of the Blue Ridge

I believe in his black dog because he had no taste for fiction,
my grandfather, no love for tricks

of the tongue (when his clever nurse/son called the stumps of his
Sugared-off legs "little whales lying beached

on the sheets," it just angered him worse). I believe in his black dog
because he was never the star

of his stories, he never saved lives or turned down all the millions
that liars so often decline.

Like the Gospels, in which the Apostles are so clearly schlemiels,
bad fishermen, running away,

dissing Nazareth (nowhere, Nathaniel calls it), they must
be telling the truth. If they'd lied

they'd have better PR.

                    So my grandfather spoke of the soul
he saw blaze into grace. He was late

to do chores for a sick neighbor, dawdling along picking chestnuts
(the blighted kind) up, and he turned

at a gooseneck. The view opened. Flames filled the neighbor's roof,

rippling

the clear air above. He lit out

running, pounding his way down the ruts—chestnuts flying from
pockets, hands, hat—and arrived to find no

fire, no damage except that the man he'd been sent to help milking
was dead.

I believe in the black

dog my grandfather saw disappear, grizzly-big, burning-eyeballed,
that loped like a dog in the path

of his headlamps. He braked for the black dog and saw it leap through,
not over, but *through* the stone wall

of a springhouse and vanish. No tracks in the dust or the mud. No
disorder among the cool rounds

of pressed butter, no gap in the milkcans' ranks, no blade remotely
like bent in the garden beyond.

In my grandfather's last days, he'd lie on the porch, stare downstreet
at dealers' dogs, pacing their plot

of packed, glabrous red clay. They had worn out the grass, mauled
the links of fence they kept running against.

They were angry as he was, and almost as trapped, and as like
to snap any hand that might help,

but they'd never, those pitbulls, etherealize
themselves, never sail through a stone

springhouse wall into infinite dusk like that vast
black dog he saw once, I believe.

A Refusal to Mourn the Death, by Car, of Dale Earnhardt at Daytona

Never, until we live again
where a girl can walk
to the basketball court unafraid,
among many pedestrians a pedestrian,
watching the red-tailed hawk
that roosts in bridge cable braid

swoop for its own delight
and hers, and play
a raptor-minded game
and walk back home that night
as safe as in the day,
the sidewalk crowds the same;

never, until we begin
to rise against what lurks
behind forty thousand poured
a year into Benz's gin,
the Bavarian Motor Works,
the mouth of Moloch Ford,

those average annual dead,
will I attempt to grieve
for him in particular.
I have plenty to mourn instead.

I slap no sticky "3"
surrounded by a blur

of specious angel's wings
on my window, no
"Gone to Race in a Better Place"
over the years of dings
scarring my bumper. Go,
buy your black t-shirts, efface

your own complicity
in his last crash. I
will admit I hold a grudge
against the whole jock galaxy,
but I didn't want him to die
and I think you did, as much

as you want to, yourselves.
You eat the shafts
of your steering wheels. Cigarette
and gas stations pile their shelves
with his face folded, half
in love with asphalt death,

a cotton/poly blend
exclusive of decoration,
because it was no accident.
It was ritual. I won't pretend
to buy into that rite, to pour the sponsor's libation
at the foot of his monument.

Living with Ballads: Sidna Allen

He mounted to the bar
with a pistol in his hand
and he sent Judge Massie
to the Promised Land:

the only mountain ballad
my mother ever sang
the years that she was raising me
on Pop Rocks and Tang,

and Grandmother thought secular
music miles beneath
her notice, so my mind is not
one Stith Thompson motif

after another, not a green
wood thick with noble felons,
no Gypsy Davies to seduce,
no Barbara Allens,

just local Sidna, late
in the murder song tradition,
coming at you straight
out of my mother's kitchen.

The Hundredth Summer of the Chestnut Blight

I lug the laundry in and wash my hands
of zinc oxide and DEET. Our crows drop dead,
the West Nile washing them out of the sky.
Snakeheads cross the Potomac, crawl on land
amphibiously southward.
                              In July
1904 the chestnut blight broke out
of the Bronx Zoo. Like some new worm, it spread
beneath the bark; it rained across the high
ridge cabins (chestnut shingles, chestnut spouts);
it starved the shoats, and bears, and gatherers
who, forced into the cities they had fed,
took sick like trees.
                              And so my grandmother's
clothesline was hung in coal soot, her whites gray,
her rooster like a rusty hinge all day.

Ghosts for Dinner

We séanced for them in a worm-wired house
whose gingerbread hung loose and crumbling,
and the trumpet vines that we called witches' fingers
broke, slow flames, into the paneless windows.
All we found were birdbones in a bedroom.

Now the love you watched plunge off Niagara Falls
and wash downstream, despite your frantic splash,
walks by our table, nods perfunctorily,
and vanishes behind a tasseled menu.
So you'll gripe for the check and walk me home
so fast I can't keep up, stomp off alone
to jog for a couple of hours, startle deer,
scare motorists, maybe, but not supernaturally

and that will not impress me. I'll stay here,
though wild boars lurk in the Black Forest cake,
those horsemen by the bar look pale and antsy,
and all the tables raise themselves and knock.
Get up to turn your chair away from her
a few degrees. And look at me. I may
be someone else's longed-for phantom. Pour
me some more wine; tell me the story; listen:
it's a dreary wish to want the whole globe ghostless.

American Viscose Plant, 1929

Few chestnuts bloom this spring. A stinking sleet
falls out of drums and ages: cider, snow,

then maple sap, it rises up the pipes
that writhe beneath her viscose-stockinged feet

and spurts into the spin room. Acid troughs,
not sugar buckets, catch it, and she jerks

it into skeins of what the girls call silk.
Sometimes she finishes: she ties, she tags,

but she is never finished. Whistles gag
the skeins; they keep on spinning in her sleep,

the thrum and breathless keeping time to works
that pull her out of joint. Acid burns

on all the boys. She must mind her touch.
Two weeks' pay docked for hangnails, or a smudge.

Clampdown

Not close friends, we've shot pool
and argued politics
across a nacho plate,
abstractly. Now the state
is making him a quick
example: out of school

and into prison. Soon.
The sentences come down
in mandatory order
and he is just the sort of
guy who stays to be found
guilty. "How ya doin'?"

sounds dumb in such dim light:
the nicotine-hazed gleam
of lightbulbs, pitchers, beer,
wiped glasses. One fact clear.
Not even the judge can free him.
Still, trying to be polite,

I ask him how he is.
Our handshake doesn't fall.
His fingers finger mine—
each knuckle, nailbed, line—
as if he might recall
a girl's hand feels like this.

Tiffanie

Her name evoked stained glass: Jonathans, Davids,
and she was both,
although who knew it? I was always loath,
when we were kids,

to stand against her at Red Rover, fearing
her strength and speed
would rip out my weak arm. She didn't need
that tomcat's ring

and threw it past all reach into the river,
then went to work
perfecting biceps and triceps. Berserk
at air guitar,

quick and loquacious at the checkout stand,
gentle braiding
my hair, she reached ahead, negotiating
our prom dates, planned

her European debut, liked to drive.
She was nineteen.
No arm could hold her back from that windscreen.
That I'm alive

and she, the stronger, swifter, dead is strange.
I never dreamed
I'd be this old, still awkward, floundering
outside her range.

Drinking Bottled Water

South of the Yangtze, swamps fester.
The exile sends no news.

                   —*Tu Fu, "Dreaming of Li Po"*

South of the Rivanna
and the Roanoke flows the Dan,
and south of that the water smells
like it should have a childproof cap.
That's where I am.

Thirsty. But the water
from the spigot stinks of must.
I wander out to buy that stuff
you drink. It smacks of decadence
to spend so much

getting slightly bitter
Appalachian "eau de source
Sweet Springs" and makes me think of all
I didn't say, last time you called.
Here comes Remorse,

thoughtfully escorting
me, my bottle, inkpen, book,

and paper towards a bench to write
a letter. Cheerful. Not about
how my hand shook,

tangled in the phone cord.
Maybe this: a landscape. Or
a pavementscape, if I describe
sky smudged against wet concrete, fronds
in planters, more

leaves reared back to strike? No.
Having found some solace in
a clot of measly daffodils
is not at all the sort of news
I want to send.

Faculty Parking Apocalypse

Faculty rustle through the gutters,
scrounging for walnuts, windbreakers stuffed,
picking their way over rusted fence,
fearless of lockjaw, ignoring the young
squatter under the rotten shed.
Some of the older faculty poke
under the bunched-up leaves furtively,
feigning a check of tire pressure. Next
year there'll be no reserved parking for
you, so you'd better be wary, sly,
subtle. And shouldn't I be hoarding
green walnut hulls, at least, for the dye?
Ink culled from sideyards, roadkill quills.

Though when stores close down for lack of stock,
so will the Post Office, phones and fax—
why couldn't someone resuscitate
the Pony Express?
                        Because horses
are lunch. See the lean muscles roasting
over a fire the mail sacks kindled?
The heart on a sharp green stick?

The Shower Curtain Swans

The shower curtain swans that float
in alternating diamond panes
of vinyl lace above my tub
take turns with reeds and lotus blooms,
serenely. Not one swan presumes
to scratch, flap, slash its beaked way out.
They soak, content, inside their frames,
each patient as a swan-shaped shrub.

No, patienter than that, because
they're fabricated. Like the drains,
pipes, pumps now laving my bare legs
with fluoridated H_2O.
I lather, happy not to go
somewhere that lacks the denouements
of water treatment. Earth contains
worms three feet long whose unseen eggs

wash into you with river-splash:
a dip, a stumbly fording, or
a thirst so strong you'll slurp up dregs.
They grow to their full meter, drift,
and exit through your nostril if
you're lucky. Else, they'll gnaw and gnash
original tracks out; they'll bore—
I've said enough. You get the picture.

What saves us from them? Chlorine. Cash.
Municipalities. A thin
membrane of tarmacs, autobahns,
and fiber optics. Artifice
in all its forms, economies
and other opaque faiths. The ash
cross fading off my intact skin
in all this steam. The frozen swans.

Disney Ride *Song of the South*

The shadow of Uncle Remus his rocker
flashes, enlarged, on the wall of the flume
but when the boats turn in their narrow tube
to see the narrator, a frog's in his chair.

The latest indignity. Turn the imprisoned
prince to a frog and the animatronic
fairy tale floats on, though deracinated,
sung to the tune of B'rer Bull and B'rer Bear,

a lie that the tourists like: not that all *shall be*
but that all *was* well, here. The ferry nears hell,
falls in its channel to false gasps from parents, who,
sure of its safety, have ponied up fare

for their daughters' amusement. The daughters can't kiss
Frog Remus. They can't even reach him across
the gap from his fireside, although his shadow
splashes over their cells to the wall where they stare.

Moved, Lost Your Number

The world is made of math, at which I suck.
It's tax and markets, physics theory, string
vibrating at the base of everything,
string deep inside each atom, proton, quark,
string singing something math says gives the world
like, ten dimensions. Music of the spheres
turns out to be the truth, though I can't prove
that, or time travel. You put any stock

in what my mom says, "Three moves are one fire,"
then twenty moves in the past eighteen years
is six point six six six . . . the sixes, twirled
into infinities, leave no scrap squirreled
away to call you with, won't say which move
was pyromania, which plain bad luck.

Fearing the Loss of My Hounds

Through January nights we'd sleep
piled up for heat and security.
On the street, Wanhope and Accidie,
    Pride and Despair
stalked, sleek and vigilant, with me
    and no one dared

disturb our stride. But now the pack
snuffles at other feet, distracted
by every sociable scrap
    its noses find.
The hounds collect more slowly back
    to me each time,

as if they don't remember who
once trained them toward perfection. True,
I don't feed them what I used to:
    lungs, liver, heart.
And that's all they want for their menu,
    me ripped apart.

Crop Cults

Recycling, grocery virtue, hopeless votes:
these rituals are how we'd save the world—
not sex in wormy furrows
to fertilize some oats,

not crucifying scarecrow hotties, once
they've mated with the May Queen. We contend
our lives are more than leaves
or lentils. That sweet dunce,

the body, understanding none of this,
still aches to blossom with the blossoming
of everything that dies.
It never heard the lies

our egos eat. It doesn't care for truth.
My body thinks of yours the way a tongue
continually roves
half of a broken tooth

it must soon lose. And it already knows
the sharp gap that the dentistry will leave.
Despite a winter of Platonic oaths,

you kissed me at the vernal equinox
and that was great but the coincidence
can't handcuff us to the grandfather clocks

of history and biology. Around
the funeral of the Loaf-King
at Lammastide, I'm bound

away to study supernatural
mechanics, make up spells too weird to die.

And so are you. No gods of husk and hull
can gobble down what we've already learned

or all the ways our tongues and fingers burned.

Living with Ballads: The Nutshell Bed

The landlord's nephew, down from college,
dreams the tenant farmer's daughter
calling him, the creek between them
running muddy, and the wind
beating apple petals in her hair,
his face, and the great space beneath
what used to be the swinging bridge
his late father kept repaired.

The posts and ropes that hold it rotted,
most footplanks broken, floated downstream,
this bridge can't join their crumbly banks.

He's rooted.
                    She steps to the edge.

What's under them? A swollen-bellied
Hereford, snagged and left in sharp junk:
sweeprakes, dumprakes, discs, drags,
plows and sickles, springtooth harrows
thick with rust, claystain, and lockjaw
making what last words she'd struggle
to utter (love? forgive?)
unspeakable.

          He shudders, discovers
himself yelling "Never!" across the creekbed,

across the bear-claw- and star-quilted bedstead
he wakes into, swearing to stop her
from trying to cross that incompetent bridge
bound to drop her.

Fire Baton

Wobbling in heels, I twirled
cold steel capped with fake pearl
down candycane-lit streets.
One parade, in Rural Retreat,
I hit Krystle Grubb. She cried.
It was that undignified.

How frozen, runny-nosed
in child-sized hookers' clothes
we'd be, I hadn't thought—
beseeching till Mom bought
me lessons. All my eyes
were dazzled that July,

the nights a still-astounding
darkness rose from the ground,
the hollows first. And just
above dark, in the dusk
of Pine Ridge, majorettes,
star-crowned in high school, met

to practice fire baton.
They knew their craft. Their wands
or brands burned at both ends
and flew. The smoothest spins
in both hands, keeping time
with drums and flames, defined

my beautiful. Not cute.
Their hands reached, resolute,
into the fire and showed
no wavering. Their code
hid rising blisters, tics,
and every cicatrix.

The Crocodile Dream, Every Seven Years

It's sepia. You're seven, padding down
the cowpath to a faraway boathouse
and out of it there leaps a crocodile
bigger than the boathouse. You turn, run
back uphill, stumble, let go of the book
(a valuable condensed book, gilt on top
of all its pages) and it rolls, it flips
right down the lake bank, hits the water. Yes,
the crocodile is gaining on you. But
you have to save it—someone else's book.
And so you fling yourself down the steep bank,
into the water, there's another splash
behind you, you hear water drip from teeth
and wake.

        You're fourteen, Technicolor, hired
to find a lost medieval manuscript
illuminated, legendarily,
with gold and lapis, buried in a barn.
Your trowel hits rock? No, box; you open up
not rotten wood pulp but a vellum—look,
the crocodile is coming. When you run
mud sucks your shoes off. You slip up a ramp
that leans into the chicken coop, hope, slide
on feathers, falling, feel the crocodile's
cold breath . . .

And say you're twenty-one, the town
you live in an agrarian stronghold:
agora, baths, surrounded by plowed fields,
surmounted by a temple built of marble
the veins of which spell words—the entire house
of your tribe's pantheon is carved with verse,
with moonlight, shadows moving in the serifs . . .

They're going to tear it down to build Big Macs
you argue brilliantly against and lose.
You pace, tear-blinded, back to that carved marble,
into the catacombs and hidden river
beneath the building. There the crocodile.
And why not let it eat you? But you run
again, wimp, and emerge on the great floor
before the altar where they're nailing up
a salad bar. You stop to catch a breath.
They drop their work. The sneeze guard shatters. Now
the crocodile stands by your side, your friend,
your terrifying ally as they flee.

If all that happened, then, at twenty-eight,
wouldn't you throw yourself at sleep, for what
must be some miracle of crocodile/
dream-self collaboration?
                              And what if
that crocodile, the crocodile of hope,
appears beneath newspaper: scum of ads
and op-eds and embedded AP wires
in a vacant office park's reflecting pool,
trash, floating fragments of a snout and skull?

You could skim out the bigger teeth, at least,
and bury them in your own skin: a sharp
pacemaker, an annoying contact
that blinds one eye, a line of curious
blue scars. And you could train for thirty-five
when God knows what fanged things will leap from you
to your assistance in the next campaign.

Magic City Mortgage Co., 1951

Approaching Wytheville's boundary sign, although
the heat's so hard the bruise-blue mountains wobble,
the well-informed crank windows up, shut wings.
They speed, if white. They've heard how polio
broke out with summer here. Half suffocating

already in the close car and her girdle,
one woman wraps a towel around the burden
of baby in her lap, to guard its face.
She tells her son to pull up his cowherder
bandanna, knots a handkerchief in place

across her husband's muffled "thanks," then draws
her own scarf down to block her mouth and nose.
Three red lights. The lap baby frets at each,
but unenthusiastically. Across
the boot-scuffed fabric of the wide back seat,

Rich scrambles from one window to the other
and spells out Main Street: Churches, Umberger
Hotdogs, two Hardwares, Beauty Carousel,
The First Virginia Bank. The bank . . . His father
blooms for him, from VP for Clientèle

to cool-eyed wheelman, masked as if they've made
their biggest heist, blown up the safe, sashayed

out to the car, a healthy gang of robbers
all smug and sweating through their getaway
from Wytheville with its iron lungs and no cure.

Idol Meat

This Christmas catalogue of sausages
and Colby cheese logs offers "Custom-made,
in the true spirit of this time of His
birth: praying hands, dramatically portrayed
in rich milk chocolate. Such a thoughtful gift!"
But I want more than that. I crave the taste
of melts-in-your-mouth godhead, no cold whiff
of pine and spruce, mute evergreens, straitlaced
and distant symbols, but the birthday kid's
far-scattered littermates praised in lost psalms.
Fearn, Dionysus, Osiris. Maenads
and I would sink our teeth right through their palms
instead of nibbling nougat-veined bon-bons.
The crunch of bone is what religion thrives on.

The Consolation of Philosophy

sounds promising: a smooth iambic title
translated from late Latin down to us.
Who wrote it? Severinus Boethius,
before getting bludgeoned to death for consulting a rival

of Theodoric the Ostrogoth, had time
in prison to hang with Philosophy, be consoled,
and leave word how.
                        Though no Ostrogothic bolt
bars my door, consolation is one thing I'm

lacking, looking for, and almost thought
I'd found when Boethius begins
to grieve about his age and sentence. Then
Philosophy steams in, overwrought

(*that* I believe). She chills fast, from berserk
to overtly officious bureaucrat
of God, all catches and backtracks—
maybe the consolation of paperwork,

but not a metaphor that really hacks it
in my book where Boethius must wait
some fourteen hundred years for engines, rails,
far-off train whistles, and an accurate

description of the Midnight Special, which
they say frees prisoners with its headlight's touch.
The beam illuminates a roach, a smudge
along the wall. The blanket! Then it's missed.

Pets, Ending with My Folks' First Dog

The whole worm farm, conceivably, outran
a fate as bait. The rest? Sunkist, Thor, Spout,
and Bill, stir-crazy goldfish, leapt and slammed
themselves free of their bowl. They just freaked out,
but what about the flattened cats and Kurtz
the gerbil, in his rolling Exer-Ball,
careening downstairs? Even feeder birds
bashed brains against the picture window. All
we hold are people now. We've learned what Dad
suspected first in '63, in his
first principalship. Any call we had
to name creatures is gone. When Dad found Dizz
hanged from the flagpole of the local High,
he found no question in that hound's popped eye.

Barry on Porch, Barry in Parking Lot

His bit-open bottle. My fairytale cup.
Barry slugging back Mountain Dew,
proud of his belt buckle: *I'll give up
my gun when they pry it out of my cold
dead fingers,* in brass. I was the young
cousin who saw him reunions and Christmas,
but when I imagined civilization
falling apart, I saw Us versus
Them. We were doomed and glorious.

He died hanging sheetrock, a father. He'd tried,
when I was a gray-lipped skulk, to save
the picnicking world from my grim appraisal.
He asked what I was reading. No enclave
of samite-clad women, no glowing ship,
no white horse went with him underground.
I remember his kneeling in the gravel
to speak to me, courtly. Glass shards all around.
The sun on his hair a kind of crown.

A Scratch

Explaining how to stick the needle
into the arm, she fumbles as if she, too,
although a librarian, forgets what to do
with records. Archaic already,
along with my overstuffed earphones,
the turntable mat,
this LP feels absurdly large and fragile.
Its tissue sleeve unwraps unsteadily,
one corner crumbling. How did people
live with such brittle arrangements of tones,
such touch-me-not ridges and grooves?
It starts. The spirals pour
endlessly into the center, thin but substantial,
and gather, pulsing, black as an oil geyser
in jubilant movies (crude-stained James Dean
and Rock Hudson in *Giant*) or
a washed-up oil spill, if you'd rather have wiser
similes. Me, I'm here to forget that.

Black as the slicked-back hair
of Eugène Ysaÿe,
pulsing out of its pomade,
thrashing as he played
this piece at his wedding feast: 28 September
1886, a glorious (i.e.,
pleasantly weathered) day. He'd posed

earlier, in sunlight, for photographs
with his bride and kin
on figured carpet dragged out across cut grass.
This work, his favorite present,
he's premiering this evening—
César Franck, its author,
too frail to travel from Paris,
too spent, dedicated and sent
his Violin-Piano Sonata.
Describe it? I'd be embarrassed;

you can look up the details in Proust.
I'm only using the music to crash, to pretend
Major and Madame Bourdau requested the pleasure
of my presence at the marriage of Louise
to the conservatory's coup
of a new professor.
Here lies the souvenir menu
for seventeen courses, tasseled, rosed,
monogrammed, scrolled, and engraved with violins.
My plumy hat roosts
with egrets and ostriches
while a fiddling-Cupid card seats me between
friends from the groom's beer-hall band phase:
Lindenlaub, his goatee newly trimmed,
and Laforgue, who scoots my chair in
carefully, not catching my bombazine.
Laforgue's quick-eyed, nervous
at first, picking at stuffed spinaches,
but the swoopy music eases

his worry over how he'll make a living
now he's quit reading for the Prussian empress.
She gave him a tea service
as a parting gift, the sole furnishing
for the walk-up in Paris.
This music licks his ears.
His book's out soon. The publisher pays.
He has just turned twenty-six
and what I hear, he hears

if he's listening. He may not be.
He may be trying too hard
to hold back his cough,
which won't get better.
Not even at *his* wedding, in three months,
with no music, on a sunless day in London.
Not ever.
Or, knowing Laforgue, he's worried
about *this* bride, just eighteen,
a decade younger than his friend
who's already toured Europe and Russia
and grown a double chin.
She's nervous enough,
and where's her spouse?
His father's getting proudly soused;
his mother (like Laforgue's) is dead
in childbed,
and he plays the violin,
swaying and stomping, all
six and a half feet of him.

Louise watches his hair whipping
like something in war stories:
the cat-o'-nine tails for deserters.
He rocks as if he's going to fall
and crush that instrument.
On his '95 tour of America
the baffled pre-Beatle reporters
will have visions of houris:
sixteen-year-old Philadelphia
girls screaming and shredding their gloves.
He'll grow old cheating on her
(though usually with titled loves),
grow old endorsing Wurlitzer
and Columbia Records.

Shortbreathed in her corset, her head
aching with all the pins bent
to hold her trailing veil,
she tells herself what does not hurt
cannot be beautiful. A good major's daughter,
she refuses to wail
until after the music. Then the floorboards
creak under the boots of her glassy-eyed brother,
home on leave, quarantined
with scarlet fever,
who escaped from his room to see her
despite his skin's blotched surface.
He stumbles at her, begging pardon
for looking so ghastly, but can't stop her scream.
She has to be carried out,

delaying the honeymoon.
The record pops and hisses.
The reserve-and-listening room
holds a rattling copier
the librarian has to smack.
Her hair is moldy blue
growing out from black
and a patron's telling her
"That piercing there's infected."
What else can I hear? Dejected
computers beep. And through
the window, an engine misses.
Roach-bait candies crunch.
Everywhere, chairs scrape.
Despite what I intended it to be,
even the music
even the music
even the music
is no escape.

An Essay in Criticism

T. Eliot and J. Laforgue
awoke one midnight in the morgue
on their adjoining slabs. Jules brushed
his evening jacket, stuck a crushed
carnation through his buttonhole
to honor his immortal soul,
then buffed the polish of a shoe
and took the stairs up, two by two,
till he was out and on the street.

Tom curled up tightly in his sheet.

Jules busked until he made enough
to buy a never-ending cup
of coffee at the Horn of Plenty Grill,
that worn utopia. No chill
could reach the heart-carved table he
shared till dawn with Leah Lee
and cream and sugar on the side.

Tom coiled in like a trombone slide.

The sun reared up, but Jules refused
to crumble like a vampire who's
shriveled at the touch of light.

Tom clamped his hands and prayed for night.

Surf with P. B. Shelley

I don't like *poems or novels. I just teach them for cultural studies.*

Dear Theoryhead:
                I'll admit that I fell out
with Shelley, for your reasons, for about
a day when I had just turned seventeen
and discovered that truckstops in European
locales were still truckstops, guard dogs still loud,
and nobody was pointing through the crowd
of tourists to my spiky, glowing heart,
nobody shouting I was set apart
for glory.
            All that day I rode the bus
and brooded on the bodyguard who'd cussed
me out, I thought, in German when I tried
to genuflect at the poet's house beside
the great lake at Geneva. Brooded on
the gulf between me—native of the wrong
class, latitude, wrong side, wrong watershed—
and Shelley.

                I identified instead
(for the first time) with Harriet Westbrook,
his first wife, and the clammy martyr's nook
she stood in, self-drowned. Condensation tears
dripped down her blank pearl eyes and limestone ears.

Resenting lords and sons of baronets
and *Dukes of Hazzard* on the TV sets
throughout the lobby of the next hotel,
the one in Nice, I didn't feel compelled
to write what I had felt. I didn't feel
a cloud of witnesses. I didn't feel.

My roommates knew the route for sneaking out
past curfew to the beach. I went along.
The cobblestones were echoing with songs
from *Rocky Horror;* lights from its marquee
and spotlit fountains led us toward the sea
or, rather, the retaining wall. Below
its balustrades was where we should not go:
unlit, unguarded water's edge. Deep black
Leviathan. We ran for it. Stones clacked
beneath our feet as we kicked off our shoes
and rolled our jeans and waded in to bruise
our ankles in the surf. Where was the shock
of cold Atlantic we expected? Rocks
or no rocks, we had never touched such warm
seawater. We went farther in.

                    Our swarm
of schoolgirls fanning out into the waves
turned into individuals. I laid
my glasses on my sneakers and splashed back
to sea, to float, a jellyfish's sac,
and then the riptide got me. Dragged along
the rocky bottom by a force too strong
for me, I tried to fight it, choked, and sank,

and rose two times to yell but only drank
when my mouth opened, couldn't see, thought I
was going to die the same way Shelley died,
like him at last. Then, with no sight of land—
this is no metaphor!—I saw a hand
reach toward me.
                    It was dim and blurry, stretched
in my direction from a distance, etched
in water. Grasping for it, I found air
and swam again. I found that I could bear
the current. I saw Nice shine like low stars
and fetched up on the shingle, retching, far
from anyone.
                    A long way down the beach
I heard my classmates calling, out of reach,
and none of them saved me.
                    No lifeguard claimed
the job. I don't know. I know who I named,
and whether it *was* Shelley, or Westbrook,
or a purgatory angel I mistook
for Shelley, my point is that someone saw
me, saved me. And it wasn't Derrida.

I scooped sea glass and gravel from my bra,
then climbed the stairs. The songs and fountains played
for me: bruised, scraped, innoculated, safe
from all you fashionistas who'd reduce
our work to driftwood, polished by abuse,
a floating empty, toothsome theory's thong—
and I intend to live to prove you wrong.

Amazed at Gray Light

Arm in flannel. Mine. A gift
I don't expect. I wake surprised
to be alive. I learned the creeps
with "Now I Lay Me Down to Sleep,"

nightly brooding on how God,
if my soul leaked when I snored,
and it improbably pleased,
would take and keep it, Vulture-Lord,

if I died, and if not, which
soul-scavenger might rip it out
to pin against a curing board
or scoop it up beside the road,

dump it into a stolen cart
for its redemption value, melt
me into mineral elements.
Uncalmed by the two decades since,

now I wake up in my dead
grandmother's nightgown, which I kept.

A Good Half Hand

In his sixth year of applying for the pension,
he wrote that *they could not know anything*
about the fistula
as it was at a place that they did not see
although he'd let the federal government
take a close look. *I was in horspital*
No. 8 at Nashville Tenn.
with measels and feaver. Had mumps in camp

I guess his messmates nursed him, too far west
for Whitman to have hovered by his bed.
Unknown cloth-wringer, bucket-emptier,
I know how dangerous mumps in a man
of twenty-two can be, how you nursed me
as well. And this genetic particle
you cooled and soothed thanks you, and if you caught
it and you had no children, if you drift
with no one's lares, be mine. Mine want help.

If I prove that my horse fell and hurt my hip
will it be any benefit to me?
If not you will doe me a grait favor to say that it will not.
I am your Obedient servent

my great-great-grandfather, whose blue tattoo
was his own name, in hopes his corpse might come

back home, though home was in Virginia where
he fought, eventually, for Mr. Lincoln.

I went through the lines in July 1863
as I have already stated

His anger thrives in me, something beyond
a trite Darwinian propensity
for fight or flight, more than environment
though in his ninety-seventh year he drilled
my mother, three, in her times tables, then
swayed out on his two canes to criticize
his grandson's fence (which stands now, overgrown).
The grapes he foraged set my teeth on edge.

I want to hack through their wild vines, dissect
this anger. It's a tangle: steep hill strung
with old foxgrapes among the hardwood, tough
enough to swing from (proto-bungee rush
that's like a fit of rage, adrenalin
alive inside me), or to strangle in.
Vines choke. Since Freud is discredited
but useful, can't Lamarck be? His giraffes
stretched out their necks to graze and had giraffes
with even longer necks. I want to say
that he was right. No, I'm no scientist.

Some kinds of work I can't do.
I can't cradle or mow, or chop a whole day.
I don't think I have been more than a half hand

since 1870 . . . I say 1870 and 1880
because those were the summers when the fistulas
were opened and I was not able to do anything.

His file ends with his widow's death, the year
my father shipped to the Korean War.
I think. I didn't ask Dad for details;
I didn't want to open anything.

Did he receive an injury while in service?
Yes. I saw his horse fall on him . . .
His foot and leg swelled up . . .
and that same night he rode as hard as he could ride
from Russelsville to Strawberry Plains
with only one foot in the stirrup and no boot on.

My father taught me how to drive. I'd dread
the other cars out early: night shifters
or hunters coming home, deer on their hoods,
and dreaded his protection, thought that he
at any minute would be ducking fire
from forty years before and running us
into an oncoming, the mountainside.
He'd grabbed my uncle's neck one time and forced
them both beneath the dash at some loud sound.
No ground was firm beneath him, or for me.

Has he received medical treatment since 1865?
They are not a family who employ a physician much.

My father balanced whole zoos of balloons
above my bedroom's curtains rods in case
the house caught fire. Alarms? We had alarms.
But if they didn't work the heat would pop
my birds and elephants. I might escape.
Years later he would drop me off at work
and sit in his pickup across the street,
on guard in case a customer attacked.

I was a jumpy bookstore clerk. I keep
an eye on my escape routes when I teach
(night English, adjunct, at a business school).
I've never cradled. I may be the end
of all their griefs that found me to inhabit.

I think he is not fit to work at all,
but he does keep at it.

The Banks of Hell

The decorator flies, in hardwood frames—
sealed tight, tracklit, expensively arranged

like Brad Pitt's backlit movie hair—mean squat
to me. The old man would have been ashamed

of me for coveting their bright displays.
His virtue was *waste nothing*. He took pains

for years before the fishes hatched to catch
our breakfast, salvaged scrap rail from scrap trains

to forge an anvil, poured and hammered lead,
and pierced it for bob sinkers, none the same,

all roughly tear-shaped, stored in mayo jars.
He built and tended compost bins that changed

our trash to rich earth, castings, ruddy bait.
I show his weights as if we weren't estranged.

Fancy Gap

If you don't make the grade, you don't make Fancy.
USE CAUTION in your approach to these curves!
She's fooled a lot of guys into thinking it's easy.
But with Fancy there's a price to pay.
Nine people paid it last year.
If you have any doubts, ask a driver who knows Fancy:
Fancy Gap Mountain descent, Route 52.

—*Carroll County Highway Commission*
and your Highway Safety Division of Virginia

1.

The poster was a fixture where we weren't
welcome, as girls: tree forts, pool rooms, full-serve
gas stations' grease pits, paneled dens with burnt
wood plaques. A guy would show he was no perv
by having Fancy up, but what I learned
from glimpsing it I wouldn't have the nerve
or words to say till more than one decade
had passed, and the bare flesh between her frayed

cut-offs and gingham halter wasn't rare.
Her shorts weren't *that* low-rise. She wore tan hose.
She had more on than fashion victims wear,

goosebumped, today. But her hillvampy pose
on prop split-rails, rope-belted, veil of hair
a gallows hood, a warning not to doze
on 52, still managed to invoke
something chthonic, older than their joke

about the grade, the curves, and Fancy's price.
Childhood was health. To ripen meant to die,
to drive on routes of bloody sacrifice
each day of a dull life, or to untie
the noose in my belt loops (against advice)
and give my body up to some doomed guy
just like the guys in Edith Hamilton's
Mythology. The local pantheon's

selection was small, though, limited to
a hard-shell, cracked, one-gendered Binity
composed of sentimental Sonny goo
and mad Dad bumper stickers; sports TV;
Hank Williams, who had died while passing through;
and, for the women, baby pageantry.
Since those were all the icons of my youth
no wonder that I felt I found more truth

in the black canvas her photographer
hung for the void Fancy arched against.
And so I built the way I worshipped her.
Remember my location: stymied, fenced,
pre-Internet. Our Methodist pastor,
hammily ignorant, had me convinced

I hadn't read somewhere but had *made up*
that story like a nerve-induced hiccup

where Jesus, playing on the Sabbath, molds
birds out of mud. Some neighbor snitch reports
his breaking two commandments, mocks and scolds
till pre-teen Jesus turns on him and snorts
and Snitch just withers up. His body folds,
completely moistureless. Around his corpse
the mud-birds spring to life and fly away.
If Pastor X had let my mind have play

among the locked bookcases like the rest
played spin-the-bottle, confirmation class
might have been a mere hoop. I might now vest
in long robes, an ordained or tenured ass
who bore her elders' code on every test.
Instead I went and broke in, smashed the glass
case doors that guarded the Apocryphal
(ascribed to Thomas) Infancy Gospel.

2.

Well, that's a metaphor. I quit the church
and lurked for fifteen years, until I heard
a poet who had done the right research
and guested on *The Simpsons* quote the bird-
and-withered-boy story. But the lurch
X left me in? I'd filled it. Each potsherd
of shiny glass and plastic that I stacked
for Fancy's altar subbed for what I lacked

in orthodox theology. Before
I stood in Robert Pinsky's audience,
his take on Thomas serving to restore
my hunger to learn Greek and confidence
in my own mind, the impulse to adore
hard-wired in me made random incidents
seem Fancy's work. A drummer I liked lost
his arm, carwrecked. The jackleg preachers tossed

that up as an example of how God
resented hard rock. I though otherwise:
it wasn't personal, not Sweeney Todd,
not hatred, but White Ladies, Lorelais,
or Phantom Hitchhikers. As Ichabod
Crane's dread of one dark stretch of road implies,
some places have toll-spirits. Fancy Gap
had mine. She owned a torn wedge of the map

of Appalachia: east to Charlottesville
(where Jefferson took over), everything
south of John Henry, north of Chapel Hill
(a basketball Parnassus)—turf stretching
as far west as Virginia went, until
in Tennessee the voice of Rachel mourning
her life with Andrew Jackson and the crowd
of rowdy Nashville muses grew too loud

for Fancy's calm impersonality.
My father said, "A pagan is a peasant,
clodhopper, etymologically;

shops Woden-Mart for superstitions, bent
on bargains, on the cheap and fancy-free
without imagining the consequent
cost in child labor, closed towns, globalized
wage-slavery." My father theorized.

I wanted solid God. We drank thin grape
juice called communion, but it lacked the kick
of alcohol; it never grabbed the nape
of my neck through my throat, ripped the fabric
of space and time, took up my female shape.
I didn't know Snake-Handlers. Melancholic,
Protestant, I wanted rituals,
and I had never heard the canticles

to Lady Wisdom written in Sirach
(Judeo-Roman-Greek-Episcopal
side-dishy scripture). Soul a limp windsock,
unlit, uncensed, inside a fragile skull,
I didn't know the Holy Spirit, *Ruach,*
is feminine in Hebrew. No hymnal
or icon had explained that. So I made
my own religion up. It called for shade

to shield my careful pallor and bruise-blue
makeup so Fancy wouldn't be irate
at me for blowing off what she could do.
It called for sacrifices: a debate
judge took points off my score for looking "too
funereal." Although I lost at State

I won two years in California with
the words I'd used to build her megalith.

3.

When I left Fancy for that fellowship
to the Far West, I thought it was the end
of her influence. She was passé, parsnip
abandoned in an old root cellar, wind
in rotten chestnut trees. The five days' trip,
with an ex-crush (now a friend's boyfriend)
on shotgun, would go far beyond her brink.
And then I looked up from a restroom sink

at Fort Kearney, Nebraska, and I saw
my collarbone was Fancy's collarbone.
The mirror showed me with her tilted jaw,
my long brown hair hers, gnarly and windblown;
my driver's sunburn made her right left arm raw
and my accent was surely her cornpone
demand for righteous vengeance. When she smiled
I saw I was a woman, not a child,

no longer acolyte, but avatar.
Still healthy. Healthier. But terrified
of how she'd use me now, me and the car
piled with my trousseau, though I was no bride.
My worldly milk crates weren't stacked up so far
that I drove blindly. I had too much pride,
was all. My Fancy system scorned compassion
the way I scorned TV and current fashion.

It would have helped me to own a TV
where meanwhile, in Joss Whedon's universe,
Buffy the Vampire Slayer learned to see
the soul in a repentant vampire, nurse
no grudges, take responsibility
for justice and for mercy. I was worse:
deciding Fancy wanted sacrifice,
I savored it like gravy with a slice

of turkey at Thanksgiving. The relief
I felt, each thing I hit! The windshield mess
of ex-bugs, sparrow in the grill? No grief.
Then all night through Nevada, limitless
jackrabbits: dead, dead, dead. The thrill was brief,
though, briefer each time, soon unhappiness.
So Fancy lost my faith. She wasn't tough.
One sacrifice was never good enough.

Beating My Head on a Curb in California

because light hurts so much—the taxi's late,
the joggers speed up near me while I wait
for my ride to the ophthalmologist
who'll treat, and call *idiopathic,* this
blue flame in my left eye. *Expect relapse.*
But first the cab has to come. Its driver chats
with his dispatcher. Language I don't know.
I get that static, though, the scanner-snow,
the lullaby of tight-lipped deputies
and paramedics Mom would play to ease
our house to sleep.

Do you know where the subject's kinpeople live?

Ask 61. I think he knows exactly
where the subject's kinpeople live.

                                        Does 61 once speak
to Subject, coming home? I make the creak
of packed snow and porch steps the only sound
as chasing Christmas lights run all around
the porch like dogs, happy and mannerly.
Out in the yard, a bright Nativity
glows, drawing in the multi-ethnic kings
or mages or whatever. Quiet sings.

I'm sick with envy, anonymity,
and wanting extradition. Are there treaties?
Have both our countries closed their embassies?

Silicon Valley, 1998

Sun beats down on the oleander,
hot cross buns and platinum rings;
the bums are arguing metaphysics,
flapping their invisible wings

down and out and then up to Ra or
Tezcatlipoca. This is not
enough, this getting the god we ask for.
I want more than I can say

here, consumption-stunned, as rich and
viscous as the cloudy honey
precipitating through my steamer,
stung and numbed by the swarms of money

buzzing from cells to palms to pagers.
Venture capital. Hacky-sack
with gold dust. I want serious wagers
on the following numbers: three in one

God, four horses pounding down
the street, twelve stars in Mary's crown,
two hands to overturn these tables;
two hands to overturn this town.

The Confirmation Gift of a Cat's Eye Headlight

Feast of Latimer, Ridley and Cranmer

My Cat's Eye guides me
over quake-cracked pavement.
Flying on my bike,
I bend like the waves bent
sliding under the bow
of the boat Bishop Ridley rode
to be tried, to his stake,
to his burning. There's no secret code.

Play the man, Master Ridley, and we shall this day
light such a fire in England as, by God's grace,
shall never be put out.

I play the woman,
not the girl,
tearing through the dark
while my church skirt swirls;
I finished off the wine
but I'm riding unimpaired;
soaring through the shadows
though the shadows say be scared,
say thread keys through your fingers
so they bristle from your fist,
chain a whistle to your thorax,

strap a cell phone to your wrist,
carry all the phylacteries
endorsed by Dick Tracy's
Crimestoppers' Club
and it still won't be enough.

They say don't bike alone
through the groves of eucalyptus
or where olive branches moan
(if you think the trees feel pity)
for the women killed beneath them.
They say drive or stay at home.

I don't own a stinking car.
Stay home? Like, I'm sure.
I'm in Salvation Army
and it's vintage haute couture.
Dressed for the wedding feast,
wine turned blood in mine,
episcopally blessed,
I am out to shine
like Latimer to Ridley,
like the moon, like Orion,
like my bike's headlight
raking the tree roots,
like every pearl spat out
by every swine.

Reaching and recanting
and reaching all the same

through the mouse and keyboard
into the flat flame,
I've been intent on ruining
my right wrist and hand,
but their metal brace proves useful
when the gearshift jams:
I slam it on the stuck shift, and
light leaps ahead
through the rosemary hedges;
I am far from dead.

Duchess

Gonna customize General Cornwallis.
Gonna strip me this salt-rusted Dodge
down through the wire and rebuild it,
get red clay and oil dislodged,

switch over to biodiesel,
fuel it with diner grease, green
soyfields, not derricks. Fix my
horn to play "God Save the Queen,"

paint Union Jacks every flat surface
no, make that the cross of St. George,
weld the doors, jump in the window,
soar over Cleveland Gorge

(Colonial Colonel Cleveland:
his troops lashed my family on stakes
for questioning his revolution;
his insurgents are county namesakes).

Congressman Cooter, you others
who show off your Generals Lee
aren't retrograde *enough*. Boys,
you want revolutions? Watch me.

Beginning with a Line by John Berryman

Dream Song 186

Them lady poets must not marry, Hal?
I'll grant we must not marry you,
not that you give us any reason to,
making yourself an (Old-Fashioned?) pain
(Wallbanger? Sidecar?) and dead.

But drop that trowel and mortarboard you'd use
to shut us up in anchoresses' cells
and I'll put down the cocktail tray
of Damocles I'm holding near your head

and sit my hips beside you to explain
not only do I want a husband whose
peculiarities are not yours, pal,

I want to be like you enough to make
some kind of music out of my mistakes.

Locket Icon

The oyster plates of Rutherford B. Hayes,
racked up, spotlit back of the Plexiglas,
although he lost the popular election,
beam democratically on diners who've
removed their hats—and not. I mind the men's
refusal to uncover. Women shiver
bare-shouldered in A/C. Six-cratered moons,
the plates, their hollows gilded, decorate
the busy walls. They bring no body food.

Some nights Maria, mopping out the stalls
in the women's locker room, sees (not a shroud,
not the dignity of shrouds) a unitard
float—footless, armless, headless—through the tile
out to the treadmills. She does not report
the poor ghost going through its repetitions
to Cephas at the desk. It is no vision;

it isn't Saint Lucia (eyes ripped out
in Diocletian's tough administration)
appearing nightly. *She*'s not shivering.
Her icon shows her wrapped in red, her eyes
re-doubled—two intensely in her head
and two that she hands to the icon-reader,
fresh and undamaged on a golden plate.

Richmond Breastworks

Our clothesline parallels the Union line
and Lee's defensive trenches end our yard.
Old bones uproot in every major storm.

I pray for my three times great-uncle, hanged
in Slabtown by his fellow citizens
because he didn't wear a uniform.

Our well draws dead men's bile. Expedience
is why I'm here. I mean to move, not dig;
I mean to let that baleful well run dry.

My uncle and his brothers "dodged about"
(their words) until it was expedient
(so Slabtown taught the rest) to take a side

but first they lived some years in mountain caves,
found wax and honey following the bees
to their wild gums. They got out of war's way

as if it were a natural forest fire,
high water they could climb above, or snow
which covers all graves equally. I say

they had a point. We should get out, not pave
or plant here. We should leave and let the dead
leaves bury dead. Find somewhere else for home.

Here flowers nameless to me, cruciform,
in hand-sized clusters, draw the bees. Somewhere
the lion's corpse becomes a honeycomb.

Montani Semper Liberi

*There are but two remedies for such a situation as this, and they
are education and extermination. With many of the individuals the
latter is the only remedy. Men and races alike, when they defy civi-
lization, must die. The mountaineers of Virginia and Kentucky and
North Carolina, like the red Indians and the South-African Boers,
must learn this lesson.*

—Baltimore Sun, *1912*

"Choose education or extermination."
Maybe you can live on taxidermy,

get by on jackalopes: the deer hinds fanged
and glassy-eyed on bar walls, body parts

arranged, unlifelike, to amuse the troops
when they come home. Or maybe stack the limbs

you cut to cordwood by the tourists' rooms.
But generally we have to go away

to eat or get insurance. We're not free.
Who am I kidding? We're not even we.

My father killed, when ordered. By degrees
he made me what the kinfolk think a freak,

so I could see the world on fellowships
while their kids still enlist to pay for school.

No old boys offered hip flasks at his wake;
No toddlers' mothers sidled up and said,

"Let's climb the Devil's Backbone like we used to,"
since that was something else we never did

as we. I wore the black I teach in, stayed
professional. The news was Abu Ghraib:

our pregnant Lynndie England with a leash
in hand, a photographic grin, the heads

that talk all talking straw men, talking trash
on West Virginia. I teach rhetoric,

so while I stuffed the funeral baked meats
into the fridge, and wrote each donor's name

I sketched my lecture on the fallacy
called *false dilemma*, as in, "You can choose

from education or extermination,
but only them, and they are not the same."

Praise

This vapid rock says *all* I have to do
is give my heart to Jesus, merely slit
the skin and split the bone. All right. I ripped
that worn heart out and handed it to you,

amazed at how it didn't hurt. And now
should I call this ache phantom pain? The glib
neglect to add what happens next—you take
my heart and carry it to your chapped lips

and close your mouth around it, like a fig,
and still you're chewing. I'm afraid you'll spit
it out like a tobacco quid to quake,
a bit of lukewarm gristle, on the ground.

Love, let me see your Adam's apple lift
the heart I give you. Swallow. Swallow it.

Lumber Room

A winter in Korea
decades before my birth
prickles through my neckhairs.
Foxhole, frozen earth,

scrawny teenaged sniper
who lives through camouflage:
my liver-spotted father,
cramming the garage

with crates of chipped beef, Spam stacks,
grosses of apricots.
I saw the old man buried;
I heard them fire the shots,

the folded flag and casings
one more load for the hoard
I sort. I'm trampling cartons
where wrath's vinegar is stored

and from my mouth come spewing
his words, like a disease.
The enemy surrounds us.
They only look like trees.

Public Transportation

you were not with me yet   you were wearing
your uniform blazer   riding the bus
and then the Metro   to work in the morning
driven through darkness   diving under
Washington's marble   warrens of warlords
into your eight daily   hours at the Holocaust
Memorial Museum   how many
winters did you
                    the winters I
slept late   learned Anglo-Saxon
left and ran lawless   lazed slammed raved
made less than a living   professing language
in the woods of the Battle   of The Wilderness
hated myself   for having a car
abandoned it out west
                    and yet
we would manage to meet   and immediately
know we were it   each other's the whole
subway could see us   our hands held
solemnly braced   on the seatback before us
in the posture of prayer   in ecstasy pulled
up through the tunnels   electric and elevated
escaping the city   the century streaming
high over the dammed-up   highways the dark and
sparkling Potomac   while over us planes rose and
somewhere beyond their glow so did the brightening stars

Living with the Bureau of Public Debt

Parkersburg, WV

Look, here is water!

Acts 8:36

Not far down the river from Wheeling,
big-name astrologers
got started, and left. The local
template of leaving's hers:

a crowned and sashed Patsy Ramsey,
mother of JonBenét,
who weeps, queened and sprung, on the diner's
wall of fame. We wait, pay,

drive home by the dark Ohio,
river in negative,
marked mainly by an absence,
though this is where we live.

We'll never be Miss West Virginia,
raptured in Final Net.
We came here like the Federal
Bureau of Public Debt
which left DC with its river

reflecting cherry blooms,
arched marble, sleek baby-joggers.
Over *this* river looms

the fire on top of the smokestacks
leaching Lord Christ knows what
all over the floodplain's stripclubs,
eating each rusty strut

that holds up the bridge, the highway—
so we all oxidate.
Behind us, the marble's melting.
Under us, pavement ate

the Mound Builders' ziggurats, meant,
like Public Debt, to link
the people with what they were missing.
Always, on the brink

of this river, the oil has pooled. It
blurred chestnut burrs, birchbark
canoes, steamboats. Now it coats,
maybe, a murdered narc,

and as for the missing people—
we come here two by two
to find them. We're on commission.
Any river will do

for holy, however poisoned,
if it carries voices. Choir
of broken things, keep on singing
"Look, here is water and fire."

Notes

Jules Laforgue (Montevideo 1860–Paris 1887) was a poet and
fabulist who influenced T. S. Eliot, Ezra Pound, Hart Crane, Samuel
Beckett, and Ogden Nash, among others. He married Leah Lee in
1886.

The description of Disney World's Splash Mountain is based on
Mark Schone's "Uncle Remus is Dead, Long Live Uncle Remus"
in the January-February 2003 *Oxford American.*

In the Episcopal church calendar, the feast of Hugh Latimer,
Nicholas Ridley, and Thomas Cranmer is October 16. Latimer's
words to Ridley as they were being executed for heresy during the
reign of Mary Tudor refer to the eventual formation of the Anglican
Communion.